To Go Left,
First Turn Right

To Go Left,
First Turn Right

A COLLECTION OF POEMS

By Cathy Nemeth Rodeheffer

ISBN-13: 978-0692551172 (CNR Publishing)
ISBN-10: 0692551174

TABLE OF CONTENTS

FOREWORD

Life takes us on many detours – unexpected circumstances, job changes, family crises, births and deaths, and a host of other surprises and disappointments. Sometimes the obvious direction is not the actual way to get somewhere.

Along the way there is only one constant – Jesus is with us, whether we perceive Him or not. My prayer is that you will learn to trust Him in all circumstances, to be with Him and allow Him to be with you. I'm still learning.

Peace be with you.

FAITH, GRACE AND PRAYERS

A CHILD BE

How can I Your child be
When worldly cares relentlessly
Beat at my door?

I must let go,
Let trust decide
And be my guide.

Let go with wings
And songs that sing
Eternal glory.

Give up my way,
And eyes must stay
On unseen Lord.

Does He now know
My suff'ring deep?
Of course; 'tis His.

And calmly will I
Go to sleep
And rest in Him.

A PSALM FOR TODAY

Dance, dance,
Dance to the Lord.
Sing and shout His praises always --
Dance to the Lord.

God has visited His people!
He has not abandoned us;
He has not left us orphaned.

He is a sure Boat in troubled water,
A Rock in shifting sands,
A Bridge across deep chasms;
He is our Life Preserver.

Though violence is all around me,
He will keep my soul safe.
Though my body be ravaged,
He will not abandon me.

Though He brings us low,
He will again raise us up.
Though He chastises,
He will again comfort us.

God's Word lives forever;
It cannot die.

Who can know the ways of the Lord?
Give all to Him,
And He will make your paths straight.

A THOUSAND WAYS

Your Love is told a thousand ways –
As slowly we traverse our days.
The fact that we exist is one,
And then the Father, Spirit, Son.

Each new green leaf, each tender stalk,
Each fragrant flower, as we do walk.
A tender touch, a kindly smile,
The one who says, "Come stay a while."

Forgiving words and peaceful pardons,
Sustaining waters, grace-filled gardens.
Creation sings; Your love song rings.
The stars, the skies, let praises sing.

Majestic mountains, roiling streams,
Icy fountains, bright sunbeams.
And darkness too, can give You glory –
More brightly shines the candle's story.

A thousand ways let hearts explore.
Your Love still gives a thousand more.

ALL ABOUT YOU

Sometimes I forget
That it's not about me;
It's all about You

Sometimes I think
I have to make it all work
Instead of letting You have your way

Sometimes I think
I have to be a certain way
Instead of just being
What You made me to be

Lord, help me to let go
Help me let You run the show
Help my heart to trust in You
Help me to get through

You're the One Who really knows
All the things I'm thinking of
My thoughts, my feelings, what's inside
There's really nothing I can hide
From You

What about my ugliness?
I need to let Your tenderness
Remove the fear
And dry the tear
Of parts of me I'd like to hide;
Oh, please stay at my side

My heart's in a jumble
All in a tumble
I sure like to grumble
And my feet tend to stumble

Lord, I give it to You
I give it to You

AND YOU SAY ...

The mom daily waiting in the car
To pick up her kids from school.
The dad going camping with his son,
Even though the dad hates camping.
And you say there's no such thing as love?

The mom or dad who cooks dinner
After a long day of work.
The kid who makes dinner
After his mom and dad's
Long day of work.
And you say there's no such thing as love?

The wife who bites her tongue
Instead of nagging her husband.
The husband who hugs his wife
After her emotional outburst.
And you say there's no such thing as love?

The therapist who listens to
Rants, raves and painful memories.
The confessor who listens,
As heinous sins are forgiven.
And you say there's no such thing as love?

The waves lapping on the shore,
The wind moaning at the door,
The flower with dew afresh,
The wild and bounteous wilderness –
And you say there's no such thing as love?

Yes, there's illness, pain and sorrow,
But there's always a tomorrow.
Yes, sometimes our hearts are broken,
But much grace -- by the same token.

A baby born in a stable bare,
A healing voice in the still, cool air,
The God-Man dying for our sins,
The God-Man living once again.
And you say there's no such thing as love?

BEHIND THE SCENES

Quietly, behind the scenes
God's love is working
As we dream.
We fuss, we fret;
Still He directs
The drama of our life's events

Like a conductor
He does lead
With perfect timing
Meets a need
Never early, never late
Life's music He does orchestrate

What seems to be a tragedy
Though deeply sad, can really be
A door to further growth, you see
Though painful, it will to Him lead

BELIEVE IN THE SEED

Believe in the seed
Though all seems stark and bare,
Though evil seems to take control,
His love will crush despair.

Believe in realms as yet unseen,
Where life is growing, yet unbirthed,
Is reaching toward the light to be,
A seedling breaking through the earth.

Believe, though all around confess
Their doubts and fears, their many tears.
Believe, though barren earth is dry --
Refreshing rains will drought deny.

Believe in the Son,
Though hidden just for now,
He, like the sun, will soon return,
And make all well somehow.

BLEST BY BELIEVING

"And blessed is she who believed that there would be a fulfillment
of what was spoken to her from the Lord." (Luke 1:45)

Blest by believing,
Blest one of faith.
Blest in her offspring,
Blest by God great.

Blest in the morning,
Blest in the night.
Blest in her dreaming,
God healed her fright.

Blest in her suffering,
Blest in her pain,
Blest in her offering
To God unrestrained.

Bless-ed be Joseph,
Her faithful betrothed –
By angel visited,
He took Mary home.

In faith going forward
On roads then untrod,
To unknown beginnings,
They gave all to God.

CAN YOU HEAR JESUS?

Can you hear Jesus?
His voice so gently calls.
I hear Him in the crashing waves,
In clear, bright mornings,
In darker days.

Can you hear Jesus calling?
He wants to own your heart.
Can you hear Him in the wind?
The fresh, cool breeze?
The Voice within?

Can I hear Jesus speaking?
Or is my heart too deaf?
Will I turn away from Him,
Let call grow dim, or --
Let Him wash away my sin?

Can we hear Jesus speaking?
And let us meet one day,
On other side,
Without our pride --
He patiently awaits.

CHOOSE

Choose to love, though you are hated.
Choose to compliment, though you're berated.
Choose to forgive, though you are hurting.
Choose to be pure, though some are flirting.

And if you fail or if you fall,
Get up again; you must stand tall.
Begin again; begin anew –
Let God's light shine, your whole life through.

CHRISTMAS

One starry night the angels sang.
The sky with their pure voices rang.
The humble shepherds looked with awe
Up at the star, and glory saw.

And we should all like children be,
Believing things we cannot see,
Expecting miracles, though skeptics doubt --
That God will surely bring about.

When He comes back He'll ask, it's true,
"Is there one with faith among you?"
So let us all like children be,
Believing things we cannot see.

COME WALK WITH ME

"Come walk with me", the Savior said.
"Leave earthly cares behind.
Leave all that comes twixt you and me --
The sin and worry bind."

His heart was aching with such pain.
He saw men struggle, strive in vain,
When in His hand He held all things --
The peace, the joy, that His love brings.

He said, "You must the silence keep,
The quietness, the inner deep.
Close every door and go inside.
To you I will My love confide."

"Each day go to the inner door
And listen as I speak, and more.
My inner peace I will impart
And make a fountain in your heart."

All men will one day bow the knee
To Him who hung upon a tree.
'Till then let us be well content
In silence, a true sacrament.

CREATOR'S GIFT

Smelly clothes and dirty dishes
Don't seem like the stuff of wishes.
Cooking meals and wiping noses
Could, in time, produce neuroses.

However, if you do your duty,
You could, in rhythm, find some true beauty.
The daily things you do with love
May lead your soul to realms above.

The simple things, seen with new eyes
May give your heart a great surprise,
When seen as the Creator's gift –
A flower, a child, a dirty dish.

CRUCIFIX

Lord, I know You rose from the dead.
You live in glory with Your Father.
But down here it seems
That we haven't heard the news.

We're still fussing and fighting –
Darkness seems so enticing.
We're still bleeding down here –
Won't You please come near?

And He did,
And He does,
And He will.

I know You overcame sin
And Your victory is sure.
You triumphed over death –
Our bonds you have broken.

But we're weak and afraid,
Our messy beds unmade.
Still thinking false thoughts
And the lies we have bought.

We get stuck in our ruts,
Wander far from Your ways.
We're still bleeding down here –
Won't You please come near?

And He did,
And He does,
And He will.

I will look to Your cross
Where my soul You have bought.
I will lift up my eyes;
Keep my eyes on the prize.

I will lift up Your name,
Trust in You all the same.
Though still bleeding sometimes,
I have You by my side.

And He loves,
And He gives,
And He walks beside us.

DON'T THROW IT ALL AWAY

Don't throw it all away ...
So you've messed up,
You've screwed up –
Keep your head up.

Don't throw it all away ...
In your anger, in your pride,
Don't allow the pain inside
The truth to override.

Don't throw it all away ...
Life's too precious,
Infectious –
God's perfecting us.

Don't throw it all away ...
God still loves you,
He'll protect you –
Don't listen to what others say:

The backbiters,
The infighters,
The naysayers,
The faith slayers.

Don't listen to the "no" sayers.

It's not up to them or you.
Surely God's word is true.
Don't believe lies
And don't compromise.

The fact that He loves you,
The truth that He died for you,
His heart surely burns for you,
You must let Him live in you.

EMPTY WITHOUT YOU

Empty without You,
Bereft of all things,
Nothing to offer,
Nothing to bring.

Only a skel'ton,
A frame without flesh,
A small, empty vessel –
Without peace, without rest.

Until You fulfill me,
Until You bring grace,
Until You infuse me –
It's from Your embrace.

You tear back the curtains,
You dissipate dust,
You melt all the misty,
You fill up my cup.

You bring into focus
What once was unclear.
The picture once blurry
I face without fear.

FACE LIKE FLINT

(Isaiah 50:7, Luke 9:51)

Lord how can I be
As strong as You?
I don't have a clue.

The Pharisee's opinions
Didn't affect your dominion --
You did what You had to do.

Will You help me be strong?
Keep on keeping on? --
The road is so long.

Set my face like flint
And don't look for hints
Of what others are thinking.

FAULTY MEMORY

My memory is really shot –
Is that man called a Ted or Scott?
Was that woman Sue or Sharon?
Perhaps she's Shawna? Rose? Or Karen?

Do I turn at Madison?
At Grant, or Tadd, or Addison?
Make a left at North Chehaney?
Daisy, Mayzie, or Allegheny?

But the place I really stall
Is forgetting who You are,
And who I am before Your throne –
I am Your child.

Just a faulty memory,
A broken circuit,
A sin, maybe.
Just a faulty memory.

Where's that paper I can't find?
Where's the bill for the telephone line?
Where's the lid for that open can?
The remote that goes on the TV stand?

Who did I forget to greet?
That lonely person on the street?
Who did I forget to call?
Where did I last drop the ball?

It's just a faulty memory,
A broken circuit,
A sin, maybe.
Just a faulty memory.

Bring it back to me, Oh Lord.
Make harmony of dissonant chord.
Remind me, Savior, strong and mild,
That I am still your little child.

.

FORGET NOT

Forget not the day
He set you free
The vision can fade
So easily

Forget not the pain
He suffered deep
So you could walk
Unfettered, free

Forget not the price
The Savior paid
The load of sin
Upon Him laid

Forget not His love
So deeply shown
Nor glorious light
That Easter morn

Forget not to love
Your neighbor near
Pass on to him
God's love so dear

Forget not to thank
And thank again
For priceless gift
Received within

GOTTA KEEP BELIEVING

Gotta keep believing,
Though so much contradicts.
People think that I'm a fool,
And devil plays his tricks.

People that I'm trusting
Seem to disappoint.
But maybe I mistakenly
Misplaced my frail hope?

Need a clearer vision
Of what God wants for me.
Don't seem to know the answers
For questions troubling me.

The road keeps getting darker --
Here's where true faith comes in.
I'm teet'ring on a tightrope,
Can't seem to trust in Him.

How long to be in exile?
How long out in the cold?
Lord, help me to surrender,
To wait upon Your throne.

Have I lost Your vision?
Has pride put me in chains?
I'll wait upon Your answer
And then be free again.

Am I disobeying?
Did I blindly fall?
I don't have all the answers;
I'll give it to You all.

Today as I drove around in the rain, I had this sense that someone, somewhere was crying deep and sobbing tears, and this poem came to me later as I sat in silent prayer at Eucharistic Adoration.

GOD'S TEARS

Today I saw God's tears in the rain
He cried great heaving sobs of sadness
The thunder was His groan
And the lightning His flashing eyes

He cried for the child who'd lost a mother
A husband who'd lost a wife
A son who'd lost his father

He cried for the prostitute who's never known true love
And the pornographer whose problem is the same
For the sad and empty ways that people grasp for happiness

He cried for the souls buried under the earthquake rubble
The people drowned in the tsunami
Those who lost loved ones in a hurricane

He cried for the victims of terrible abuse
And for their abusers

He cried for the soldier wounded in war
And the one who had wounded him

He cried for the woman whose lungs were burned
By an unknown allergy to a medication --
She's now in an induced coma to help her heal

He cried for your sins and my sins
And for the hearts hardened like ice
That will not come to Him to be thawed

Today I saw God's tears in the rain
And I asked Him, "When will the suffering end?"

I did not hear a voice, but the thought came …
"Perhaps … when you forgive the one who has hurt you
When you call or write or visit a sick friend
When you pray for those who have no one to pray for
them
When you bring laughter to someone who is sad
When you are kind to one who has not been kind to you …"

Then I saw God's smile in the sun
When the rainbow appeared, He said,
"See, I give you hope: I keep my promises."

He smiled at the child laughing in the playground,
At the husband and wife embracing
At the flowers that stubbornly poked through the snow
He smiled when He saw His creation
And saw that it was good

GRACE

'Tis only by the grace of God
That somehow I am still alive.
He has allowed me one more day;
What e'er the reason, He can say.

He suddenly will come to me
With touch of joy and comfort great.
I did not ask nor earn, and yet,
By grace His love and mine are met.

When emptied self is filled by love,
Earth's cares transformed from heav'n above,
Just by Your grace can it be known,
Love so amazing now is shown.

GREAT AND AWESOME

Great and awesome, mighty God,
You who made the heav'ns and earth,
And every soul that comes to birth.

We do not understand Your ways,
Oblique to every mind are they.
How often we misspend our days.

We struggle, strive, to keep alive.
We fight, we hate, offense do take
'Til understanding comes – too late?

Your mercy, grace, so fathomless;
Your justice, anger, so restrained,
Until the time You have ordained.

Your patience for us wayward souls,
Your love expressed a thousand-fold --
Infinity we now behold.

How do we, You comprehend?
How, small soul, your ways to mend?
His mercy triumphs in the end.

HE WILL COME AGAIN

I'm waiting for that day
When He returns
In bright and shining glory.

I've got to tell the story --
How He loved me all the time,
But I -- confused in mind.

He always walked beside me,
Tried every way to guide me,
But there was no way I would see.

Couldn't grasp His story.
My ears were stopped, and surely
My eyes were blinded too.

I walked in deepest darkness,
Lived life in blackest starkness --
My heart was frozen.

Now He leads me through the night.
I look to Him for light,
Like a little child.

HELP ME LOVE YOU

Jesus, help me love You;
To live for You each day,
To put my life into Your hands –
With faith keep fear away.

Let me see the beauty
You made for me each day,
To recognize Your glory
In things that come my way.

To see You in each moment,
In clouds and burning sun.
To see You in disguises
That all around me come.

To see Your plan so awesome;
In joy and sadness praise.
To see you both in drudg'ry
And pleasant things each day.

To put my trust completely
In Your plan so great.
And help me tell Your story
So all can contemplate.

HIS HEALING

Head hanging
Shoulders sagging
Couldn't be bragging
About my mood

Soul searching
Heart hurting
Forever turning
To face a wall

Dawn breaking
Light changing
God saving
My empty soul

Joy filling
Heart thrilling
Restlessness stilling --
He does it all

I NEED YOUR SONG IN ME

Lord, I need Your song in me
To still the noise around.
And keep my heart in tune with Yours;
Let me be heaven bound.

In daily work, in drudgery
Let spirit sing Your praise.
That I will let Your gifts to me
My heart and mind amaze.

Let not my soul so weary be
That I neglect Your painter's stroke --
Let all the tasks ordained for me
A masterpiece evoke.

And soon a heavenly chorus will sing --
An orchestra and heavenly choir.
With joy and thanks in perfect tune,
And Spirit's joyful fire.

[Written during the California drought of 2014 and during the Ferguson, Missouri, riots.]

I DREAMED THAT IT WAS RAINING

I dreamed that it was raining
And streets were wet again.
The cars went by
And gave a sigh
As water splashed on them.

I dreamed that it was raining
And children laughed aloud.
With gleeful hoots
Their muddy boots
Through puddles gaily plowed.

I dreamed that it was raining
And clouds burst forth in flood.
Their waters calmed
The violence strong
And peace could now be found.

I dreamed that it was raining
And living water sped
From streamlets high
To rivers dry --
The thirsty land was fed.

I dreamed that it was raining
And black made friends with white.
The past was healed,
Their friendship sealed,
With harmony in sight.

I dreamed that it was raining
Upon the wasted land.
The thirsty earth
Could now give birth
To many seedlings grand.

I dreamed that it was raining
And cleansing tears were shed
O'er mem'ries deep,
I now could sleep,
Could rest upon my bed.

I dreamed that it was raining
And God forgave my sins.
He calmed my fears
And dried my tears,
And I could live again.

I'M DANCIN' AGAIN!

I'm dancin' again!
Through the pain,
And through the tears,
I'm dancin' again.

Because the dead are raised to life,
And peace will come through fearful strife,
Because the wrong will come to right --
I'm dancin' again.

Because my heart,
Though so confused,
Is slowly, gently being infused
With grace, and truth, and light.

Because the pain is for my good,
Because He's always understood,
Because with God I really could --
Learn to dance again.

Because the cross will cure my sin,
Because He'll bring me peace within,
The peace that silences the din --
I'll dance again!

Inspired by the following quote:

"Jesus deigned to teach me this mystery. He set before me the book of nature; I understood how all the flowers He has created are beautiful, how the splendor of the rose and the whiteness of the Lily do not take away the perfume of the little violet or the delightful simplicity of the daisy. I understood that if all flowers wanted to be roses, nature would lose her springtime beauty, and the fields would no longer be decked out with little wild flowers. And so it is in the world of souls, Jesus' garden. He willed to create great souls comparable to lilies and roses, but He has created smaller ones and these must be content to be daisies or violets destined to give joy to God's glances when He looks down at His feet. Perfection consists in doing His will, in being what He wills us to be."

St. Thérèse of Lisieux

LIKE A DAISY

Like a daisy in God's garden,
Not rose nor lily fair,
Like Leah to Jacob's Rachel,
No beauty to compare.
Yet Leah brought forth Judah,
Of whom our Lord was heir.

And all the kings and queens of earth,
And those who lack in means,
Come to this world with nothing,
And leave with naught, it seems.

Whether you be famous,
Or by the world unknown,
His purpose you must surely find,
Unique to you alone.

ON JAGGED CLIFF

On jagged cliff
I stand in balance.
For love of God
I take the chance -- yes.

Or stand at start
Of tunnel dark,
And enter on
A somber lark.

I walk the rope
Twixt light and dark.
Upon His word
I must embark.

I cry and cry,
And moan and sigh,
And then He says,
"On Me rely."

And like a child
I take His hand,
Beginning now
Adventure grand.

RESURRECTION

Because He died, I am forgiven.
Because He lives, I have hope.
Because He loves me, I can love others.

RAMBLINGS

On darkened roads I wander
The wilderness I chose.
Or did You choose it for me?
I do not know.

The one reality I know
Is God's love for me.
I cling to it like a drowning rat.

I thought God had forgotten me.
Through lonely times
I didn't even like myself ...

He began to show me His love,
Hidden by my deafness and blindness.

He patiently shows me His beauty.
He asks, "How did you like My sky today?"

He sends me waves that crash and smash
Through the cobwebs in my mind --
Through the fog
That threatens to overwhelm me.
He never gives up on me.

So sad, my soul,
But let it be;
My victory will come.

I wander blindly down an unknown road,
Knowing only that You love me.

> (If I could only comfort
> Your aching heart.
> What joy to know
> That I had touched another.
> Then my own sadness
> Would have a purpose.)

I'm in a dark place now.
It's the outer outline
Of a colored piece of glass
In a stained-glass window.
Without the outline,
The picture would mean nothing.

> (So mute, I cannot even speak.
> I never learned to tell the truth
> In a way you could understand it.
> So I babble on,
> And it makes no sense to you.)

I will yet rejoice --
The window will be beautiful,
Made radiant in His love.

RETREAT

I've retreated to a quiet place;
Just need my space.

Too many things are coming at me;
I cannot think.

Different voices, different choices;
Who's telling the truth?

All sincerely, intensely believing –
Is someone lying?

Focus on Jesus, He'll never leave us.
Our mighty God!

[Written after a friend's niece was murdered.]

SHATTER THE DARKNESS

Shatter the darkness,
Bring searing light.
Break all the bondage
With holy might.

Rend all the ramparts,
Strongholds of fear;
Bring understanding --
With wisdom draw near.

Strengthen our weakness,
Courage now give.
Cleanse with Your Spirit
Our madness and sin.

Strike now our enemy,
Make him forlorn;
Let all his strongholds
Be tattered and torn.

Give us Your power;
Your spirit embue.
Without You, dear Jesus,
There's naught we can do.

SING A SONG TO JESUS

Sing a song to Jesus,
Raise your voice up high.
Tell Him that you love Him,
That for Him you'd die.

Pour your heart out to Him,
All your secrets bare.
He will not reject you --
Trust Him if you dare.

Give your heart to Jesus,
Fall in love once more.
Life will be adventure --
New things you'll have in store.

It may not be easy;
Many trials may come.
But life for you will deepen
Until the race is done.

SO GREAT A SAVIOR

Oh, so great a Savior
Who shed His blood for me,
Who loved beyond all measure
And hung upon a tree.

Who washed the feet of creatures
With dirt and sin defiled,
Who saw in me, a sinner,
A soul to save worthwhile.

Who in most-desperate persons
Sees holiness and good;
The thief, the whore, the tax man
With Him to heaven could.

O holy One and mighty
So great a price You paid --
Endured abuse from sinners
And in the grave was laid.

Oh, mighty, glorious Savior,
Who from the grave emerged
Victorious over Satan,
And gave my soul new birth.

SING ANYWAY

Many tears I've often cried
Some sorrows lived and more just seen.
I've heard of many tragedies --
Of heartbreaks, pain and misery.

But never mind,
I still must sing
'Cause otherwise the pain would crush,
And anyway I have a King
Who has a deeply healing touch.

Illness, sickness, death and doom,
Madness, jealousies and gloom.
Accidents not meant to be;
Misunderstandings -- let them be.

But anyway,
I still must sing,
'Cause otherwise the load's too great,
And anyway I have a King
Who in the end will sadness take.

Don't even know the reason why
Such sorrow seems to seize my soul.
Another's pain can often rend
My heart -- and then --
It takes a while for it to mend.

And still,
I will keep on the song,
'Cause otherwise there's too much pain,
And anyway I have a King
Who in the end will vict'ry gain.

So sing with joy,
Let sorrow flee --
The King will have the victory.

SPEECHLESS

How can I speak of Your love, Lord?
Your patience to people of earth?
How do we understand Your ways?
And grasp Your incredible worth?

How can I tell of Your mercy?
Express your gentleness great?
How to tell how You saved me?
From tortuous, miserable fate?

How do I shout from the rooftops?
Your patience long-suffering, kind?
How to continue in silence? --
In You, endless wonder I find.

How to heal misunderstanding?
How to love those who hate?
How to forgive all the heartache?
My unrest let me finally forsake.

SPIRIT'S FRESHNESS

The misty morning,
The sea-salt air,
The flowers blooming,
Without a care.

A fresh beginning,
Day starts anew.
Our spirits filling
With purest dew.

The freshness waning
As day grows old.
With faith sustaining,
We must be bold.

When sadness threatens,
When fear seems strong,
The Spirit will come
With fresh'ning song.

SWEET MELODY

I heard the bird's sweet melody,
And in his song he said to me,
"I have pure joy because I rest
Upon the Savior's gentle breast."

"I do not worry, nor do I fear.
He holds me tenderly and dear.
Sure plenteous food He lets me find
And every need He does provide."

I saw the beauteous flower's raiment;
Its colors were from heaven sent.
Its beauty gave the Father glory,
And of His love did tell the story.

I saw a man with head bowed down,
His consciousness of death allowed
Him not to trust, instead to worry --
To be too anxious and to hurry.

He raised his head, began to see
The flower, the bird in melody.
He asked forgiveness, and in awe,
He praised and thanked Creator God.

[Written at Michele's request.]

THE ENEMY OF LOVE

The enemy of love is cynicism,
Put-downs, mocking criticism,
Unforgiveness, holding grudges,
Being other people's judges.

The enemy of love is fear --
Freezing feelings tender, dear.
Building walls of strong protection
To shield oneself from hurt, rejection.

The enemy of love is sin,
Disallowing the Spirit within.
By Satan's power we are molested,
Until forgiveness is requested.

THE LIGHT

On the mountain top I saw
A vision of a would-be world.
Some people seemed like angels,
Beings of light-amazing;
Not God, but God-infused.

The world seemed to glow
And I wondered
If I looked different too.

God smiled at me
And suddenly
I knew:
He loved me too.

I took the light down to the valley
Hoping others would see –
Most did not.
My face did not glow like Moses;
How silly of me.

I must let Your light shine through;
If others do not see, let it be.
Let me not hide the light
Out of fear.

The light, the fire
Burns within me.
I only need to fan the flames
By spending time with You.

No one can quench this fire;
Once lit, it burns forever.

THE WANDERER

Lost in the desert,
Mouth parched and dry,
Wandering always,
Wondering why.

Shadows approaching;
Must keep at bay --
Walk toward the sunlight;
On the path stay.

Desperate searching,
Cold from the chill.
Is all this wandering
Really Your will?

Increase my faith,
My sins please forgive.
Make my path straight,
So I can live.

Are we rich in any way? It may not be material things ....

THE RICH MAN

Invited in, I shyly stood,
Not knowing if I really should.
You see, I had so much to lose --
A fancy coat, expensive shoes,
My pride of life, my love of booze.

[The door too small to take it all ...]

Undecided, there I stood,
But I could see beyond that door
Some happy people, singing all.
But I would almost have to crawl
To get within that little hall.

I'd have to bend, might have to kneel.
My fear, my pride, I sure could feel.
I turned around, dejected still.

I wandered long; I wandered far,
But in my mind could see the door
Still beckoning, still off'ring hope.

While wandering, I lost the shoes,
The fancy coat, my taste for booze.
Somehow they didn't seem to give
    My soul its very-needed lift.

[My feet were calloused; my soul was bruised ...]

I lost my pride; where did it go?
The things I'd thought; they were not so.
    Inside-out, it seemed my life;
Continuing, but filled with strife.

Then humbly came I to the door.
I knelt; I crawled, into the hall.
With tears of joy I was received,
And my own tears, my fear, relieved.

TRINITY

Not a fable, not a story
Is my King the Lord of Glory

Not a dream nor fantasy
Is the Blessed Trinity

The First, Who out of nothing made
The stars, the sky, the little babe

The Second, He is God's own Son
Who died for sins of everyone

The Third, He is the Spirit of life
And gives us power in the fight

VAST AND DEEP

How vast and deep, Your love it seems;
I cannot comprehend.
I wake, I sleep; but still Your love --
It never seems to end.

I cannot grasp, nor can contain
Such love beyond my scope.
And yet, without this love of Yours,
I surely cannot cope.

You fashioned every part of me,
You thought of every cell,
You made a creature so unique,
And made me very well.

And only love was your desire --
You did not need this creature weak.
You made me out of Love's pure fire,
And ever still my soul do seek.

You choose the wretched, lost, and ill,
And lift them up from dire state.
You change the heart, transform the will,
And do a new creation make.

How can I grasp Your love divine?
How can I give this soul You've won
Back to You, as I only now
Begin to know and learn to love?

UNDERNEATH

Underneath
We're all the same.
We all have joys,
We all have pain.

Beneath the darkness of one skin,
Or other color, the same within.

Beyond philosophies and quarrels,
You still need love, you still need hope.

Beyond the arguments and wars,
Beyond each sea, beyond each shore,
There lies within, there lies within
The same capacity for sin.

Beyond the politics of power,
Beyond the ticking of the hour,
Beyond the violence, the hate --
Each one is hoping it's not too late.

Each heart is yearning for God's love,
Each face is looking up above,
Sometimes not knowing, ever turning,
Never showing, but always searching.

Will you be the shining light?
Will you take up arms to fight?
Not metal weapons, swords or guns,
But prayers and actions – the violence shun?

Will you, dread foes with love engage?
Will you forgive the one you hate?
Will you lay down all your life?
Refrain from selfishness and strife?

Yes, we must die to our own way,
We must to God in silence say,
"Lord, in my life, You'll have your way."

WALKING ON WATER

Go out onto the water;
Yes, take the first brave step.
No doubt cause you to falter,
Nor look in water's depth.

Climb up onto the summit;
Go forth one step each time.
Fear not, and you'll not plummet –
The view will be sublime.

Reach out to many hurting,
One person at a time.
Though you may not feel worthy,
God's love from you must shine.

Go forth into the darkness,
Though you don't know the way.
There's death and there is starkness;
His light will be your stay.

Keep on, though you are weary;
Let eyes look up above.
Your goal, which is God's heaven,
Will heal your heart with love.

HEAVEN

A FAR AND DISTANT LAND

There is a far and distant land
Of which we all must dream
Where tears turn into diamonds
And laughter runs in streams
Where children play along that shore
And dance in bright sunbeams

Where hungers are all satisfied
And wounds long held do mend
Where strife and sin are but a dream
And troubled thoughts at end

There is a far and distant land
To which we all must look
And if I knew it very well
I'd write it in a book
'Til then, while cares take up our time
Our hope is in that land divine

I DO NOT SPEAK YOUR LANGUAGE

I do not speak your language;
I only speak in rhymes.
Perhaps I'm from another world,
Or from another time.

Perhaps I am an alien --
My brain is wired wrong?
I cannot speak too plainly,
I'd rather sing a song.

I'm from another universe,
Or country far away.
Struggling bravely to converse --
Withhold what I could say.

I'm singing songs to Jesus;
I'm praying in my mind.
My eyes are turned to heaven --
That country so sublime.

So please be patient with me;
I need to learn to see
Reality, and firmly be
Both here and heaven bound.

REQUIEM

Rest calmly now
Your troubled brow
Let Lord of love
With peace endow
Your soul which wandered
On this earth
Allow Him now
To give new birth

To distant lands
You now must go
And leave behind
All that you know
A greater glory
You will find
Of joy and love
And peace sublime

SOMEDAY

Someday I'll walk in heav'nly lands,
By crashing waves and sunlit sands,
Shall walk beneath an azure sky,
On grassy hills and meadows lie.

No more will furrows cross my brow,
No more my worries back to bow,
No more to let my peace be stirred,
By frowning face or angry word.

Then will I let God's love enfold,
Will tell His story bright and bold,
Will shine forth with His glorious light,
My weakness showing forth His might.

LOVE AND FRIENDSHIP

DELICATE FLOWER

Swift Runner met Delicate Flower,
And under the soft silver moon,
He asked for her hand in marriage.

Their canoe flew swiftly
Over the waters
Gliding smoothly like oil
On the glass-still lake

The storm came unexpectedly
And when it was over
He could not find
His beloved Flower

She comes to him in dreams
On soft summer nights
Gliding on the perfume
Of mock-orange flowers

DID YOU EVER?

Did you ever prod a sea anemone?
Well, that's me.
If you come too close,
I scrunch inside;
I hide.

Did you ever touch a little snail?
That's sometimes me.
At slightest touch,
They scrunch inside;
They hide.

Did you ever see a flower in early morn?
Sometimes that's me.
They open wide
To the morning sun.
They're having fun.

Did you ever hear a songbird sing?
That could be me.
They tell the world
Of all their gladness,
Their springtime madness.

Did you ever feel the softest breeze?
That can be me.
I'm whispering
My love to you
And friendship true.

ENDLESS LOVE

If I could only give my heart,
Tell those I love how much they mean.
And anger only shows I care;
To disagree does not mean hate.

If I could give a sunlit song,
A calming balm, a hand so strong.
If I could tell each one I meet
How precious is their soul, and sweet.

One day I'll learn to speak my mind,
To honest be, and still be kind.
To let myself be hurt once more
And tell the tale of endless love.

FALSE ENEMY

I thought you were my enemy
But someone had told me lies about you,
And so it seems,
Someone had told you lies about me.

We went around in a fog of falsehood
That seemed so real
Because the fog was all around us.

Then the light
Began to break through
For me, for you.

The mist still mystifies
But it's getting thinner.
Slowly the sun
Is burning through.

Are we just relating
To ideas of each other,
Or who we really are?

If I could see
With eyes divine,
I would not believe a lie.

JUMBLED DREAM

I fell into a dream and screamed.
I fell into a vat and laughed.
I flew around the sky and cried.
I prayed, and then my fears were stayed.

I broke into a song and longed
For peace within my troubled heart.
I wrote this poem with these words
To stop the threat of life absurd.

I felt the wind against my skin.
I felt the peace well up within.
I tried to give you all my heart --
At least, I made a running start.

I sang the song of always-love.
It flew in air, like peaceful dove.
The Spirit came from up above,
And told me what His secret was.

I fell into a new romance.
It made me jump about and dance.
Alas, 'twas just a thing of chance --
A fluke, a spark, a happenstance.

And now I see that nothing lasts,
Except the love born in my past.
The Love that brought me from the womb,
And will be there when I'm entombed.

LOVE KEEPS FIGHTING

In the driest dirt, in the poorest soil,
Love keeps fighting an endless war.
Amidst abuse, and toil, and war
The battle rages forevermore.
In countless houses, in countless homes
The struggle rages, the end unknown.

Will love win out, will fighting cease?
Will kindness, gentleness increase?
Will patience gain a new foothold?
Will holding tongues show that you're bold?

The real struggle is in your heart –
Will pride and selfishness depart?
Will wanting your own way soon end?
Will you on Jesus' love depend?

So ask yourself at each new day –
What can I do to end the fray?
When disagreements sure must loom –
Must listen to the other's tune.

The fight again is in your heart –
It's not that differences won't start,
But how we handle different tunes;
Will it be harmony or ruin?

MISTAKES WERE MADE

Mistakes were made,
It wasn't my fault.
The only problem
Was that I got caught.

I never lie,
I don't prevaricate,
Well, sometimes, maybe –
I fabricate.

Shame, embarrassment,
Cover-up, hide.
It's only human
To feel guilt inside.

To let it go,
Confess the deed.
Must own your problem,
And then you're freed.

POEM AND EQUATION

Though not so black and white,
In general:

You are the scientist;
I am the poet.

You are the measurer;
I go by the ebb and flow.

You like rules and laws;
I like intuition.

You reason;
I emote.

Two ways of looking at reality --
Both are needed.

Both poem and equation
Show the beauty of creation.

PRECIOUS JEWELS

Precious jewels are the people I love,
Or those God has sent me to learn to love.
Maybe I'm not there yet,
But He's teaching me.

Starting out like rugged rocks,
We jostle each other.
Bumping, scraping,
Shaping, being shaped.

Don't hide in a corner,
Or you won't learn.
You won't be shaped
Into the beautiful sculpture
God created you to be.

Sometimes the jostling hurts;
Sometimes we hurt others.
Not always meaning to, but it happens.
All the while something beautiful is happening,
If we allow it.

How beautiful is polished stone,
Shaped by rapid water
And river rocks.

SLIP OF THE TONGUE

How could I do that awful thing,
With words to bite, with tongue to sting.
How could I cut off other's words,
To thus imply, "You are absurd."

With ease I fall and don't suspect
The words I say might have effect.
And sure myself have often known
The hurt of words from other's tongue.

So, grant us, Lord, we do implore,
Our tongue to hold, our words to store.
And let instead encourg'ment come,
So we'll have peace when day is done.

THE FOREIGNER (TO MY MOTHER)

How did I come unto this place,
This foreign land of foreign tongue?
Strangers, strangers, everyone --
I don't fit in and don't belong.

He sent me to a foreign land
To people that I did not know.
His goal I did not understand
I had to plant new roots and grow.

Doubts and fears -- they crowded in.
My faith was fragile, but survived.
Mistakes, delusions, sometimes sin;
And still He kept right by my side.

My soul was bitter; my way was hard.
But oft' a glorious light broke through.
He sent companions to my side;
His friends and mine His love showed true.

And now I know His purpose great --
His plan He had to orchestrate.
This life is not for foolish pride,
But that His name be magnified.

Heaven is my real home,
"The only goal," I said three times,
And sent my children on their way
With blessings in the Father's name.

And so life's circle has come full:
The morning, noon; then day is done.
The life that from the darkness rose
Goes back to meet the Father's Son.

THE THIRD LOVE

Crystal waves break
On sloping sand --
You hold my hand.

I didn't see it coming.
A different love
Broke into my life.

First puppy love,
Then wedded bliss --
And now this.

Quieter, deeper.
Long years together
Made us stronger.

The third love
Is the best so far.

[One day I was out walking and I kept thinking of my friend, and this poem came to me. Later I found out that was the day she'd gone into emergency surgery.]

TO MARTHA, MY CHILDHOOD FRIEND

Muddy puddles
And balls of clay.
Rain-slick streets
And friends at play.

We wandered 'hoods,
And built big forts.
We played in sprinklers
In polka-dot shorts.

We drank from hoses;
We played hula-hoop.
We ate salty seaweed
On the neighbor's stoop.

We dreamed big dreams
Of solving mysteries,
We made up rhymes
With hickory-dickory.

We played recorder,
A kind of flute.
We sat on doormats
Made of jute.

On Halloween,
We made a haul.
A load of sugar,
Ten pounds in all.

We played outside,
'Til it was dark.
We'd stay all day
At the neighborhood park.

We played mah-jong
And shared our tomes.
Your encyclopedia
You always loaned.

I don't know where
That world has gone.
But as time travels,
It's just begun.

[Headline: "Seven Dead in Drive-By Rampage Near UC Santa Barbara"]

WOUNDED WORLD

Wounded is this world
By sin and strife.
Unhappy people,
Unhappy lives.

Dissatisfied and --
At an unpeace.
Looking for something;
Needing release.

Compassion is needed --
Understanding, love.
God's intervention,
Grace from above.

Love to your neighbor,
Give compliments.
Brotherly friendship,
It only makes sense.

Build up; don't tear down.
Encourage; not bully.
Don't take it personally;
Grudges are silly.

If I can now
Take this advice,
I'll be one person
Making things right.

YOU ARE LOVED

*[Written while watching the movie "Waste Land",
about garbage pickers in Rio de Janeiro.]*

You are loved
in Jesus' name.
It's not your riches,
nor any fame.
Not what you did,
or didn't do,
What things you own,
or your great school.

It's not how many
friends you have –
No boyfriend, girlfriend? --
Don't be sad.
Lift up your head,
Because you're loved.

YOU'RE BEING JESUS TO ME

O'er many years,
You saw my tears,
You listened without judging.
You laughed out loud
At silly jokes,
And with your smile you hugged me.

When you forgive,
When you are patient,
When you are "merely" listening,
With gentle words,
You just encourage,
As tears in eyes are glistening.

I do not know your suffering,
What comfort to your mind I bring,
I don't know what you're going through
But just the same I'm telling you --
You're being Jesus to me.

NATURE

GLORY-DAY GIRL

Blackberries bursting
On briarly bushes.
The sun beams so bright,
Her eyelids it pushes.

The bees they are buzzing,
The butterflies bright.
The flowers are splashing --
A glorious sight.

Picturesque painting --
The colors of nature.
She laughs and she dances;
The glory-day makes her.

A song she is singing,
Her soul it takes flight.
When sunshine is happy,
She laughs in delight.

IN THE SILENCE

Rushing, roaring water
Speaks to me of
Better places, wild and free

Cool, quiet woods –
Only the birds and insects speak,
And their incessant hum
Is a calming song

Waves of warm air
Billow like a curtain
Waiting for the sunset
To let in the coolness

Watch what you say –
This is a holy place
Where God meets man
In the silence

ONLY A SHADOW

Today I see Your beauty,
An ever-changing sight,
But really just a shadow –
Creation mirrors Your light.

The wonders You have fashioned
Are merely slightest glimpse
Of Your majestic glory,
Your awesome pow'r intense.

The roaring river waters,
The waves that rise and fall,
The quietness of shallows,
The soaring eagle's call.

But sure Your greatest wonder,
The utmost height of all,
Is how You love Your creatures,
Though oft' we gravely fall.

SOUND OF THE RAIN

In the sound of the rain,
I found my peace.

It shut out the voices
That told me lies.

It helped me let go
And just be me.

It was strong and steady
And calmed my heart.

It told me that God
Was there for me.

Creator of the rain,
I thank thee.

SPRING EMERGING

Bird songs billowing from the hedges,
From meadows, grasses, trees and sedges.
Twitter, toot, hoot, and tweet,
Their song and melody so sweet.

Flowers timid peep from ground;
Will the warmth still be around?
Frogs in creeks at night do croak;
Parents take walks with little folk.

The sun can warm us as we walk,
But clouds are good to cool us off.
Still a chill in morning air,
But new life mitigates our cares.

THE GARDENER

I cling to clods,
I dally in dirt.
I dig up the sod
And wait for God
To perform the miracle
Of seed to plant.

I work in the sun,
The cold and the rain;
Inclement weather
I do not disdain.
From dirty fingers
I do not refrain.

I witness a miracle:
Every day,
The miracle of life
Is on display.
When it's time to plant,
I do not delay.

Such wondrous things
I do perceive:
The seed, the seedling,
The first new leaf.
Continually the new thing grows;
When it will stop, God only knows.

Amazing thing,
That on its own,
The seed into a plant has grown.

THE SCOURING SEA

How much the ocean lifts my soul,
And fills my lungs with freshness full,
Clears cobwebs from a cluttered mind,
Breathes in new life, leaves cares behind.

In symphony the waves do roar,
They crash upon the sandy shore,
Wash, scour and sift the detritus,
And leave essential things for us.

Oh ocean, as my God so good,
Please cleanse my heart; I know You could.
Remove all bitterness and strife
And grant me peace for all my life.

UNDER MIND

(Psychology, Therapy and
Mixed Emotions)

A BALL OF YARN

There's a ball of yarn
Inside my chest;
Something struggling to get out --
Don't know what it is.

Sometimes I feel
Like a mute
Who can only
Make noises, but not speech.

I had a voice once
And I will again.
Only time will tell
The story,
The mystery,
So well.

A DIFFERENT ROAD

So happy for you
That you've found your way,
But while I'm still waiting
I hope that you can say,
"Take courage, be strong.
It may be short, it may be long.
Don't lose heart, make a new start
Every day."

While you smile in triumph,
Don't forget the ones
Who still have a long way to go.
They arrived late to the show;
They didn't know the things you knew
When you were young.

For some, one step
Takes tremendous strength,
While you have already run the race,
Or you're near the end.
Of course, it takes grace.

Don't let me wallow in self-pity.
My gifts may be different than yours,
But still God-given.
Please just recognize
That to win the prize
It's a different road for each person.

But I must thank you
For who you are.
Although it's painful to see
Someone who's always ahead of me,
How else could I grow?
Thanks for taking the time
To share your wisdom sublime.

A LITTLE GIRL

A little girl can sometimes sing,
Can flit about on angel's wings,
Can dance with fairies, now unseen,
Can be so sweet, or make a scene.

A little girl loves daddy's whiskers,
She doesn't mind that they are ticklers.
A little girl sits on his lap;
Head on his chest, she takes a nap.

A little girl has wondrous dreams --
On unicorns she'll catch moonbeams.
She gathers starlight in her hands,
She dreams of being a princess grand.

A little girl in time grows up.
She gives up dolls and other stuff.
But every woman's heart can tell --
Inside, her child is living still.

AN ACHE INSIDE

There's an ache inside
Which we try to hide.
A great abyss
which can go amiss.

An empty hole
Inside your soul,
Where something cries
"Do not deny!"

Where children's eyes
Are full of wonder.
Where dreams and schemes
Are torn asunder.

In which we know
There's something more.
A cavern, cave
In which we rave.

And if you want
That hole to fill
You must bow down,
You must be still.

CAN'T KEEP THE POEMS IN

Can't keep the poems in,
The words that sing
Of suffering
And joy extreme.

They make me sane,
Help put a frame
'Round jumbled thoughts
And pensive knots.

They make a fence,
Repel nonsense,
Build peaceful scenes
And help me dream.

The words are strong,
They build a bond.
They help express
Love's fruitfulness.

CLEAR AS MUD

The things I thought
Meant quite a lot
Have come to naught.

I'm from another world.
My life is quite absurd,
Except for God's good Word.

It doesn't seem to matter.
There's nothing here to flatter.
I'm only getting fatter.

No feedback nor response,
No nod nor mere nuance,
A muddy ambiance.

This feeling of confusion --
Can it be delusion?
I need a blood transfusion.

CRITICISM

When anger festers,
When negativity soars,
Don't you know it's an open door?

To worms and snakes,
To thoughts that take over
And make you squirm.

Don't let that creeping thing
Take over.
Start over.

You don't deserve,
You shouldn't serve,
The god of criticism.

JUST ONE MORE PERSON
(IN THERAPY)

I'm really mad
You're not my dad.
And not a friend --
Perhaps God-sent?

But anyway,
It's so frustrating.
Can't talk to you --
I'm always waiting
For just one word
Of encouragement,
Like an email or a funny joke.

A weird and forced relationship
In 90 minutes has to fit.
I'd like to think you think of me
But I'm not your kid or friend, you see.

Just one more person in the line;
Next please; there just is not the time.
This whole thing sucks
I have to say,
But beggars can't choose;
That's just the way.

LIFE GOES ON

Life goes on, life goes on
Even when you thought it gone,
Even when you tried so hard
To shut it out and want it done.

It has a way of oozing out,
To make you cry,
To make you shout –
Life goes on.

I wonder if I really tried
To fully live and not to hide --
I wonder if I laughed and cried,
Would life go on?

If people knew my inner thoughts,
Would life go on?
If sometimes I would just express
Some tenderness,
Would it embarrass?

If honestly I said my piece,
And calmly thoughts I did release
With love, respect --
But would it still
Cause some regrets?

Does anybody want the truth?
Or would they rather have deceit?
Would they want to sugar coat
And keep our friendship on remote?

And even I
Might tell a lie,
When fear is crouching
At my door.

But while there's life there's hope;
It's not a joke.

.

MOTIVATIONS

When I turned my face away from you,
Maybe I just didn't want you to see me cry.

When I didn't speak,
Maybe I was afraid I would yell at you.

When I laughed loudly and annoyingly,
Maybe I needed attention.

When I hurt you with my words,
Maybe I hadn't dealt with my own hurt.

When I seemed to ignore your pain,
Maybe I hadn't let God heal my pain.

When I got violent,
Maybe I was extremely frustrated,
And no one had ever taught me how to deal with it.
No one was there to guide me,
To help me find better ways to deal with anger.

When you listened to me,
I began to heal.

When I asked your forgiveness,
I began to heal.

NONSENSE POEM

I had to change my mind;
My thoughts were too unkind.
They rattled round
Without a sound,
And injury profound.

I had to change my ways;
I had to give up praise
Of others to me --
They might eschew me --
Can't let them undo me.

I had to give up pleasure
As if it was a treasure.
Although the feelings
Are appealing,
They don't bring healing.

I had to give up dreams --
Nightmares, visions, screams.
Not good for health,
Going 'round with stealth,
My brain they melt.

I had to give up.
I had to let go.
I had to change.

MOVIN' ON

The room's still a mess,
The world's in distress,
Bill's haven't been paid,
There's no sun, just shade.

But I'm movin' on, movin' on.

Sometimes feel depressed,
And maybe just stressed,
Feel I can't get a grip,
And the news gives me fits.

But I'm movin' on, movin' on.

I'm finding new joy,
I don't need a new toy.
I'm letting it slide,
Going to take a joy ride.

And I'm movin' on, movin' on.

Gotta choose to feel good;
Can't just do what you "should".
Make the best of this life;
Let go of the strife.

And I'm movin' on, movin' on.

Let others go argue
Tryin' to prove that they're right.
Prayin' to accept it all --
Letting go's the best fight.

Let's get movin' on, movin' on.

Can't let the world kill you,
Demands all around -- still you
Do what you can, and just
Keep movin' on, movin' on.

NOT AS ADVERTISED

I didn't sign up
For this lousy trip.
"First class" was promised –
"Third Class" says my ticket.

Sunny skies predicted;
It's started to storm.
Lots of companions?
Not at all; I'm forlorn.

Friendly co-travelers?
Instead I get abuse.
A smooth, easy road?
I say, "What's the use?"

But on the horizon
I now see a sign
Of blue skies coming,
Of happier times.

The road – it's what you make it;
The load – it can be shared.
The weather? You can take it.
Rain or sun? -- Be prepared.

Companions or foes –
Could it be my choice?
Just listen as you travel
And hear a still, small voice.

PART-TIME DAD

I don't need a part-time dad,
Someone who tends to make me sad.
Someone to whom I only speak
But two, three hours of the week.

Someone whom I have to pay
To be a friend and to parley.
Just sits there listening; not much advice,
That I should pay at such high price.

Someone who I cannot call
At day, at night, when in a stall.
Someone who I cannot hug;
When it's time to leave,
I have to shrug.

I guess I better learn somehow
To let my anger go, and now
Have got to see I'm just as bad --
There's probably someone
I'm making sad.

PIECES OF A STAINED-GLASS WINDOW

My life is in pieces
Which you intentionally broke
Like pieces of a stained glass window

Shattered my once solid illusions
Broke up my long-held,
Wrong-held
Beliefs

I'm breaking up
Cracking up
Shattering

In a brilliant white light
I'm falling

Will you catch me?

PERFECTIONISM

Well, you just can't be good enough for some people;
Their standards are higher than a steeple.
No matter what you do, your intentions are cruel;
At least that's what they think of you.

No matter how you try, they're still gonna cry
That you've been unfair, that you really don't care.
That you're surely a jerk, and your ways just don't work.

Well, maybe they're right; it seems to be my plight
To be misunderstood, no matter how good.
Yes, it must be my fault; looks like guiltless I'm not.

Okay, I'm not perfect; I just can't live up to it.
Your standard, that is. I'm just not a whiz
At following your ways -- I'm in a daze.

So it's time to chill out; quit making a shout
About things that don't matter; stop all the chatter.
Let's give it a rest; it'll be for the best.

SWEET SLEEP

Come sweet sleep --
Let eyelids tiredness reap.
Let all my cares be put to bed --
Tomorrow they'll be there instead.

Snores and sighs and murmurings;
Tossings, turnings, vivid dreams --
Let the shade of sleep be drawn
Until another day's new dawn.

Where does my soul go in my dreams?
Unconscious in a sense I seem,
Yet living in another sphere
Of fantasies and fleeting scenes.

While in its slumber, mind does mend
The conflicts that my heart do rend,
And somehow then when I awake
A fresh perspective do I take.

THE BRAT

I really am a spoiled brat –
Lazy, and I live on fat.
Lots of money, lots of time –
Like to grumble, like to whine.

Though I'm better off than most,
Of my problems like to boast.
Like to grumble, like to whine –
For others' problems have no time.

Need a dose of gratitude,
Need to get a better view,
Need to buckle down and work –
Not be such a lazy jerk.

Need a Savior who can say,
"I love you, like you, anyway."
Need to let His gracious love
Rain down on me from up above.

THE MELTDOWN

I heard your words --
They seemed absurd.
Inside my mind
They twirled and whirled.
What you said's
Not what I heard.

They festered in
Mind's darkest place.
No logic there
I could embrace.

They bubbled, troubled
My thoughts and then,
They went in circles --
'Round again.

Next time I hear
These words that trouble --
That torture, fester,
Twist, and bubble ...

I'll take a moment
And ask myself,
"Why not just put them
On the shelf?"

THE PAINTING

I walked into a painting,
A seascape rich and grand.
On one side were the scudding waves,
On other, emerald lands.

Above the waves, so aptly hung
A rainbow of all-colored hues;
Like fairy bridge it spanned the waves,
And hung 'neath cloudy view.

I could not tell which land was real --
The painting or my troubled life.
The peaceful setting did give lie
To oft-felt turmoil, strife.

The vibrant air, the soft sea spray,
The colors of the flowers' hue,
Did stir within my weary heart
A joy and peace anew.

I walked into a painting,
And will I ever know
Which land is real, which fantasy?
Seems only time will show.

THE PROUD ONE

My life is perfect;
I have no fears.
No qualms nor worries,
No sighs, no tears.

While others fret
And have their crises,
I do not care;
I take my own ease.

I did it all
With my own sweat.
No help from others,
With no regret.

I don't need God;
He's for the weak.
My own vainglory
Do I seek.

But there's one thing
I must admit.
It's kind of lonely
Where I sit.

THE STORM

A burst of tears fell,
Like rain after the threatening clouds.
There had been rumblings and flashings --
Groanings --
Like a woman giving birth.

I smiled at you,
But you did not smile back.
I gave you a flower,
But it fell unsniffed to the ground.

THE THERAPIST

It isn't easy
Telling you all my sins and fears
To cry those tears
To admit I'm not all here

I don't know if there's a better way
To share
I couldn't find the person there
When I needed them

I tried to hide
I even lied
Without knowing it

I lied to myself
And tried to pretend
I was someone else

But you found me out
Somehow I shouted out
My inadequacy

Must it be this way?
I really can't say

Perhaps I'll learn
To discern
Those who are safe

And then I'll say goodbye
And cry
For another farewell

WHILE I WAS BUSY

While I was busy
Feeling self-pity
I missed the joy of the moment

While I was busy
Being offended
I missed a lesson I could learn

While I was busy
With jealousy and envy
I missed my abundant blessings

While I was busy
Feeling so bitter
I missed the sweetness of creation

While I was busy
Being self-righteous
I missed the grace that I could give and receive

While I was busy
Feeling you'd attacked me or my beliefs
I missed God's unconditional love for me

While I was busy
Holding onto my anger
I missed God's unconditional love for you

WHO I'D LIKE TO BE

In your eyes
I'm just a little girl
I'll never be an equal
In your eyes

It's the way it has to be
I've got to learn to set me free
By letting go of you

I have to learn to rejoice
In who I am
Instead of who I'd like to be

ODDS AND ENDS

ALL HALLOW'S EVE

All Hallow's Eve – called Halloween,
When ghosts and goblins can be seen.

The night before the Saints are celebrated,
Pumpkins carved and finely calibrated.

The candy orgy makes you porky.
The sugar high makes kids fly high.

Yet still a candle brightly burns.
Let faith fight fear and tricks be turned

To acts of love, to kindness bold,
To light that conquers fears of old.

ANOTHER DAY

Alarm goes off --
Get up and pray.
Starting out
Another day.

Cold water splash
Upon my face,
On Adam's daughter
Of human race.

Do morning chores
And then get dressed.
Give husband hug,
And cheek caress.

And then we both
Go out the door.
Another day
Begins once more.

INTERSTATE 5, CALIFORNIA

Lemons, tomatoes,
Abundant in trucks.
Big 16-wheelers
Between which we're stuck.

Windmill propellers
Sixty feet long;
Convoy of army trucks --
Men look so strong.

Low-riding race cars
Police were escorting,
Garlic aromas
And cattle cavorting.

Tall tandem bicycles
Built for a scream.
Cruisin' on the highway --
Was it a dream?

ON MAGNOLIA STREET

On Magnolia Street in Mountain View
My nose was tickl'd by morning dew.

I kicked the seed pods as I passed,
Though squirrels found them great repast.

The pods had ruin'd my mow'r twice,
Left on the lawn against advice.

So if you walk in Mountain View
Please stop and do pick up a few.

PHOTO CREDITS

All photos by Cathy Nemeth Rodeheffer, except:

"Retreat" – photo by Michele Alice Coldiron –
Bow River Basin near Canmore, Alberta, Canada

"A Little Girl" – photo by Thomas Lee Rodeheffer

"All Hallow's Eve" – photo by Thomas Lee Rodeheffer

ABOUT THE AUTHOR

CATHY NEMETH RODEHEFFER was born in 1954 in Oakland, California, the third of four living children of emigrants from Hungary. Growing up in the San Francisco East Bay, she delighted in the outdoors, singing in the back yard and pretending to be a bass player. She developed an interest in gardening and poetry at an early age, and enjoyed making mud pies and marching in the rain in a yellow oilskin raincoat with friends.

After initially writing some poems as a young teenager, her pen was silent for many years. Through the grace of God, the love of others, and therapy, she began writing again in 2010. While the poetry is healing for her, her prayer is that others will be touched and healed through these words that come to her at unexpected times and places.

Cathy is now married, resides south of San Francisco, and has two grown children.

www.ingramcontent.com/pod-product-compliance
Lightning Source LLC
Chambersburg PA
CBHW071858020426
42331CB00010B/2575